How to be Witty

(For Someone Who is Not)

The definitive manual to being funny, clever, witty,

and owning it in social environments

Table of Contents

Introduction

I want to thank you and congratulate you for downloading the book entitled, "How to be Witty (for someone who is not): The Definitive Manual to being funny, clever, witty and owning it in social environments".

This book contains proven steps and strategies on how to become a humorous person. It informs you, the reader, about the basics of humor, its various classifications, as well as skills that must be developed to make people laugh.

Here's an inescapable fact: you will need the assistance of humor to improve your social acceptability. Only by understanding how humor works in a social setting can we increase our likeability among our peers, colleagues, and friends.

Our experience has made us realize that humor is an essential part of our social interaction and life becomes easier for people who possess the ability to make others laugh. This enables them to develop strong social connections and in return positively affect each aspect of their lives.

If you do not develop your ability to bring out the smartest puns in the conversation, then you are going to miss out on the many opportunities that life has to offer. A joke is the smartest way to break the ice with a potential employer, a witty comment can make people remember you even though they do not know you, and a funny statement can help you meet your special someone.

Learning the art of humor has become more important than ever. These days our interactions are becoming more and more distant and impersonal. The advent of technology in our lives has made the person on the other end of the call, chat, or messenger basically a nobody. This emphasizes the need to be capable of generating humor in any conversation.

It's time for you to become an amazing conversationalist by adding the little puns in your conversations. It is time that you reform your life by building your vocabulary, boosting your intelligence, learning how to use puns, and by mastering the art of conversation. All of this is explained thoroughly in this book.

Chapter 1: Social Acceptance and Humor

Forces that drive our behavior in various social settings have been the object of research for over a century. If things are to be kept simple, our social interactions are majorly a pursuit to "belong". This desire to belong has played an essential role in the survival of our species.

There was a time when human beings were not the strongest inhabitants of this planet. The earth was populated with animals that possessed physical attributes suitable to survive the harsh environment and they dwarfed the Homo sapiens in strength, agility, and size. In order to survive it was necessary for the humans to organize themselves in groups. This collective living enabled them to survive against the odds of long childhood and weak existence, without any fur and claws, and provided the humans of those times a sense of security and protection.

With the advent scientific transformation and discovery in our lives, the situation has changed. In today's world, a world where we no longer live in caves and the provision of basic necessities of life are sponsored by the state, an individual can survive in isolation. However, we still tend to group up to feel safe and protected.

Maslow described it as a need for belonging and love, which may not be strictly essential for our survival, but has a major role to play in our day-to-day interactions. Our behaviors are motivated by our need to be accepted. This acceptance determines what kind of people we will interact with, what kind of personal and professional opportunities will be available to us, and whether we will be included or excluded from the groups of our choice.

Rejection

On the other end of the acceptance paradigm is an equally important, but opposing force, rejection. It is not difficult for us to recall those moments in our lives during which we felt rejected. It might be when we were the last to be picked for a dodge-ball team, or a group of friends did not inform you about their plan to hangout. The only thing common between such experiences is the anxiety and the feeling of hurt which follows and that is the only reason this bad memory stuck with us for all these years.

The fear of this rejection is another factor that motivates us to try harder and be accepted. It might be surprising for the one hearing it for the first time, but the truth is the pain of being rejected is similar to the pain of any physical injury. The effects of social rejection can be witnessed in the transformation of emotional, cognitive, and physical states of a person. Violent and aggressive behavior, anxiety, depression, jealousy, and sadness are just a few of the consequences that result from social rejection.

The impact of social rejection can be directly observed in poor performance on intellectual tasks. Social rejection also has physical impacts on a person. Their sleep quality is reduced and their immune system does not perform as well as a person with a more social acceptability.

Despite the fact that we are born alone and we die alone, there is no way we can exist for the entire length of our lives alone. Acceptance into a group, a community, a race or a creed is essential for our existence. The importance of social acceptance can be understood by the impact it has on a person's self-esteem. It is through how others interact with us that we are able to define our worth.

Constant rejection makes a person feel unwanted and unimportant, which can further lead to psychological issues, thereby affecting the quality of our lives, personally and professionally. It is through forming groups that we are able to manage our issues and problems.

Behavior Modification

We all have heard about support groups for patients battling cancer or any other fatal disease, for individuals who are dealing with alcohol and drug abuse, and for those who have a difficulty dealing with their anger. The basic theme behind organization of such groups is that human beings desire to be associated and within such association, troubled individuals find the strength they need to cope with their problem.

It is not that we need to be accepted in to a group only in times of trouble. We constantly modify our behaviors, most of the times subconsciously, just to be accepted in our group of peers, colleagues, or friends. This modification in our behaviors is our tool for avoiding rejection. We agree to do things, which we would otherwise be not doing. We keep ourselves from saying things that we firmly believe in just because the group we are trying to be accepted into would not be comfortable hearing our ideas.

This modification in behavior comes naturally to some of us. These people are more sociable, are welcome in any gathering, and have strong and vast social networks. However, some of us do not have any clue why they act so awkward in the presence of others and what makes them less sociable. In order to answer this question they need to reflect on the tiniest detail of their behavior and to become more sociable they need transform themselves.

For some people getting accepted into a group may seem to be an arduous task. It is because our behavior is a reflection of our personality and changes in personality do not come easy. However, it is not a lost cause.

The easiest way to social acceptability is to possess the ability to generate humor. It is evident that humor is a form of communication, which can be used to easily become more likable and acceptable in any social setting. Humor is the most common icebreaker in a conversation. It tends to bring together people with diverse tastes and beliefs to share a laugh. The most important thing people can do is to make other people laugh. These people are welcome anytime. Thus, it makes humor an important key to attaining social acceptability.

Chapter 2: Basic Elements of Humor

As the previous chapter concluded by emphasizing on the importance of humor to gain social acceptability, this chapter focuses on the important aspects of being humorous. We have to consider that being humorous does not only improve our chances of becoming acceptable in a social gathering, it also helps to reduce stress as well as cope with pain.

Six Elements of Humor

To understand the basics of humor one needs to look at the six basic elements of humor, which are target, hostility, realism, exaggeration, emotion, and surprise. The purpose of explaining these elements is to help you focus on the aspects that would make your jokes funny.

Element #1 - Target

The basic purpose of humor is to criticize. However, criticism is usually not acceptable and is rarely appreciated. In order to make it acceptable and appreciated as humor, criticisms must be disguised as entertainment. The focus of any criticism must be a specific target or else it would lose its essence.

The selection of the target is the most important factor because unless your audience can relate to the target, they would not find it funny. The focus should be on selecting the right target for the audience. The selection of the target must reaffirm the preexisting hostilities and prejudices of the audience. By taking advantage of these preconceptions the humorist challenges the status quo and tickles the funny bone of the audience.

Element #2 - Hostility

The most important role of humor is that it counteracts the hostile feelings that are brewing inside us. In our day-to-day lives we interact with numerous people and not everything goes according to our wishes. This may be due to the pressures exerted by someone in authority or it may be due to group differences.

It can be an issue of money or family, whatever it may be, the hindrance in achieving our goals gives way to feelings of hostility towards some target. Confronting the target directly may jeopardize our lives, thus, we make use of humor in venting out these feelings of hostility in a manner that generates laughter instead of trouble.

Element #3 - Realism

Truth indeed sets us free, but we all know that the pragmatism of our lives do not allow us to openly state everything we find true. There are considerations to be made and repercussions to be accounted for, before we let the truth out. Humor comes in handy at times and allows us to be true to the core. Jokes mostly address the bitter realities of life, which we commonly ignore. The truth in humor does not only allow us to be free, but also provides a ground to connect with the audience.

Element #4 - Exaggeration

Stating exaggeration as a basic element of humor just after realism, raises many eyebrows. On one hand, it is necessary to relate jokes with reality, but on the other, it is equally important to build up a story around it that sounds funny to the audience. Let us call it a humor license to exaggerate the narrative, just as we allow the poetic license to expand on realistic themes with soaring imagination and unabashed metaphors.

Element #5 - Emotion

If you have ever had a chance to sit in through a comedy show you would have noticed that before every joke the comedian tells a story. He draws up the whole picture allowing the audience to connect and to anticipate. This anticipation builds up the tension and anxiety of the crowd.

Let us think of it as a balloon, the more details the comedian adds to his story, the more this balloon inflates. The successful execution of the joke demands that the comedian enchants its audience in the emotion of the story and make them anticipate about when the balloon will burst.

Element #6 - Surprise

This last element is the most important one. Humor is more like a magic trick, you ought to deceive the audience, guide the astray, and when they are least expecting it - draw the punch line. Surprise is the primary reason behind the crowds laugh. It can be considered as mentally pulling the rug out from under the audience. For that to happen, we have to fool them to stand on it in the first place. If they see you preparing to tug on the rug, they will move. This element of surprise must be used with caution. If you over use this element, the audience will get wise and won't take the bait.

Building Your Sense of Humor in 6 Steps

These elements of humor come in handy when one is trying to execute a joke, but what about building a sense of humor? Is it acquired? Or is one born with this natural gift? Well, laughter is universal, but humor is acquired.

One needs to work on it, seek out the funny side of every story, and then develop a narrative that doesn't bore the audience while also ensuring a hearty laugh at the end of it. In order to get there one needs to follow this six-step guideline to enhancing your sense of humor.

Step #1 - Learn to laugh at yourself

Your story is the only story to which you are going to get a firsthand laughing experience from. This experience puts you in a position to dissect and find the humor in it. If you are able to find the absurdity in your own circumstances, you will also be able to find the humor in life.

It is mostly about perception. Your circumstances can either put you down or you can take a hold of your fears and embarrassments by turning them into funny stories. This would allow you to have the strength to laugh at what life throws at you and will enable you to share this funny side with your friends.

Step #2 - Laugh at others (within reason)

It is natural for us to laugh at anyone who is in an undignified and embarrassing situation. This is because laughter is an expression of superiority over another individual who is facing an embarrassing situation.

In order to develop a sense of humor we need to observe others and laugh when the situation allows. However, one should keep in mind not to hurt the feelings of others. This observation will allow us to add more detail, exaggeration, and at the same time make our story more realistic when we are telling a joke.

Step #3 - Keep an ear out for "benign" humor

For something to be funny, it has to be out of the ordinary. It must break the expectations of the audience and should be a violation of anything that is considered normal. According to Peter McGraw and Joel Warner, authors of *The Humor Code*, the best jokes are benign violations.

This benign element needs to be added to separate humor from scary. The violation must not be too dark, offensive, or threatening because if that case, it would take the funny out of the situation and the real purpose will be lost.

Step #4 - Learn a variety of jokes

Like every other skill, telling jokes requires a lot of practice and effort. To get the laughter that you want, you have to learn strong jokes and learning jokes is not about memorizing the lines. It is about timing, the precise amount of pause that is required before the pun, is what holds the whole joke together.

Always consider your audience before preparing jokes because the joke has to be understandable before it becomes funny. A "software engineer joke" might kill at work, but in a group of football players - it will simply be weird.

Step #5 - Actively look for a "laugh" every day.

In order to get the funniest jokes out of life, you must always be ready in capturing the funny part of life. This can only happen if you are actively looking for a laugh each and every day of your life. It is just like a photographer is viewing the world through the viewfinder just to capture that perfect moment. If he is not ready, he misses the moment. In order to find your daily dose of laughter you should add it as an item to your daily to-do list, actively search for something humorous, and do not mark it off until you one.

Step #6 - Laugh at death.

Anxiety is a killer. It stresses us and takes our mind from enjoying the real pleasures of life. The two main sources of anxiety are illness and death. The best way to deal with anxiety is to laugh it off. This is why death is the object of numerous jokes, cartoon, and comedy.

If you can help people take a break from this ever-burdening anxiety, then you sure are going to be a popular comedian. In order to make others laugh at death you need to first change your own perceptions and learn to laugh at death yourself. The moment you start finding death humorous is the moment you can start joking about it. And, if practiced to perfection, you can help others get rid of the anxiety that death brings by sharing a few laughs with them.

Chapter 3: Classification of Humor

Traditionally humor is considered as the quality of being amusing or comic. The importance of humor in our social lives and the basic elements of humor have been highlighted in the previous chapters. This chapter builds up on our existing knowledge about the basic elements of humor and the six-step guideline for enhancing our humor.

Understanding humor requires that we discover the fundamental classification of humor. This understanding of the various types of humors is an essential component of developing an overwhelming sense of humor that will enable you to impress the audience by using the most suitable form of humor.

Pun

The most common form of humor is pun. A pun is defined to be a sort of joke, which uses a word with multiple meanings or a word of similar sound, yet having a different meaning. The multiple meanings that can be derived from the pun make it hilarious. It is often used to deride or mock someone.

Innuendo

Innuendo is classified to be a form of a joke, which is indirect and often considered as a derogatory hint. The innuendo always has dual meaning. The evident meaning of an innuendo is usually innocent and supports the speaker because he cannot be blamed for the hidden meaning, which is only discovered in the mind of the listener. To achieve its dual meaning, an innuendo usually takes the support of a pun.

Malapropism

In the cases of pun and innuendo, the speaker uses a correct word to generate humor from the alternate meaning of the word. But in the case of malapropism, an incorrect word is used in place of a word with a similar sound.

This exchange of words usually results in a nonsensical and, most of the time, humorous utterance. Malapropism can be either intentional or unintentional. This form of humor derives its name from the renowned character, Mrs. Malaprop, in the play "The Rivals" written by Richard Sheridan in 1775.

Spoonerism

Spoonerism took its name from the name of an Oxford professor, William Spooner, who is credited for making this type of humor famous. The defining characteristic of spoonerism is the switching of corresponding consonants, vowels or morphemes between two words in a phrase. More than two words can also be involved in the transposition of sounds. A spoonerism can be done either intentionally or unintentionally by the speaker. However, the end result is a hilarious phrase.

Mixed Metaphor

As the name suggests, mixed metaphor is a combination of two or more metaphors or clichés. The defining aspect of mixed metaphors is that this combination is not in harmony with the speech. It derives its amusement from being absurd and out of place. Most of the mixed metaphors are accidental and haphazard.

Joke

A joke can be either practical or verbal. The purpose of a joke is to either amuse the audience or generate laughter. The most important aspect of a joke is the punch line, a humorous ending. The punch line is always preceded by an amusing story. Both of these components of a joke are equally important. The story catches the attention of the audience and guides them in to a specific thinking pattern, which will ensure that the punch line sounds humorous. A punch line is the quick and witty sentence that makes the audience burst into bouts of laughter.

Extended or Running Gag

An extended or running gag consists of an amusing situation or a line that is repeated throughout a story. It derives the humor from its repetition. This repetition can be either appropriate or inappropriate for the situation in which it exists. A running gag sets up the audience to expect another occurrence of the joke - the bait of the humor. But, what happens is that, the speaker substitutes it with something else - the switch of the humor.

Shaggy-Dog Story

A shaggy-dog story comprises of a long story or an anecdote narrated extensively. This narration is marked with irrelevance of the details and repeated phrases that hardly make sense. The humor in a shaggy-dog story is driven from an absurd anti-climactic punch line. During a shaggy-dog story, the narrator or the speaker leads the listeners by making them expect that the ending would make some sense. Most of the times the speaker will top the narration with a pun, thereby making the listeners laugh at the absurdity of everything they have heard. To sum it up a shaggy-dog story is a pointless story, which is a joke in itself.

Parody

A parody is one of the most recognized forms of humor. It is widely appreciated and people find it extremely amusing. The audience limits the humor in the parody, as a parody is a comic imitation of something or somebody, in which the performer exaggerates and mocks the original. It can only work if the audience is familiar about the subject of the parody. It makes sense only to those who can relate the parody act to the original. Hence, by comparing the performance to the original, they find the humor in parody.

Satire

The best way to differentiate satire from other forms of humor is by identifying the intent of humor. A satire is focused to shame individuals, corporations, government, or society at large, with the main goal of inducing improvement.

It takes the help of abuses, follies, shortcomings, and vices to mock and ridicule the target. This attack on the target alerts the audience by making them aware of the problems that the satire aims to address and in this way it builds up a foundation of reform. It is considered to be the oldest form of humor taking its roots from the ancient past.

Irony

Irony is a kind of humor in which the joke lies not in the literal meaning, but in that which is totally opposite. It intends to ridicule in an unkind manner, especially when the outcome of a situation is opposite to that of what was initially intended. Irony does not seem to be funny for an outsider or one who is not aware of the situation.

For the one who can comprehend the irony is the one who is aware of the situation and can fully realize the contrast between the aimed outcome and the real one.

Overstatement

As evident from the name itself, an overstatement is to state something in exaggerated terms. The funny part of the overstatement is the exaggeration itself. The exaggeration is unrealistic, easy to catch, and amuses the audience by its creativity.

A speaker makes the audience laugh by telling them that he is so hungry that he could eat a horse. He exaggerates his hunger to an extent that it crosses the realm of reality and makes it funny for the audience.

Understatement

Just like overstatement, an understatement derives its absurdity by deliberately minimizing whatever is being spoken about. The audience is amused at the comparison because they understand the real situation and the unrealistic contrast tickles their funny bones.

Statement of the Obvious

This form of humor takes advantage of a situation being unworthy of comment. The audience considers a certain situation normal or expected, but the speaker makes it hilarious by putting it in a form of an observation. The key to making a "statement of the obvious" hilarious is in delivering this statement in an expressionless manner. The seriousness of the speaker is what actually makes it funny.

Exclusive Humor

Exclusive humor is audience-based. It is characterized by being funny only to a particular group of people and when thrown at an audience outside of that group, the latter may fail to understand it. This is mainly because they have never experienced things that are specific to that group and are usually unaware of the jargon that is being used.

It is similar to the case of a writer who can understand the jokes relating to publication deadlines or an editor's anguish. For other people, there would be nothing funny in that and thus, it will be an exclusive humor for the writers club.

Absurdity

Absurdity has its roots in the obvious absence of any logical reasoning. This absence of reason makes the statement foolish, ridiculous, and for sure, funny. It is used to make people laugh and can also make a sophisticated point. While using absurdity as a form of humor, it is advised to oppose reason or common sense. Use fantastical and whimsical ideas and betray the harmony of the surroundings.

Sounds in Humor

It is a common for humorists to take help from the sounds of the verbal utterances of words. This helps add fun to any narrative simply by adding an extra layer of pleasure that compounds or intensifies the existing humor.

This can be done by repeating of the beginning sound of words, which is called alliteration, by using the word for similar consonant sounds called consonance, by words that imitate or sound like their meaning called onomatopoeia, and by rhyming giving the extra edge to the absurdity contained within.

Chapter 4: Skill Building

Being born with a considerable sense of humor is a great gift. It naturally gives a person an advantage in gatherings and social settings. It helps one to be more likeable, socially accepted, and be an apple of the eye amongst friends and family members. However, if you are the person who was not gifted by birth with a command over humor, there is nothing to worry about. Like all other skills, it can be learned through practice and by addressing certain aspects of your personality building.

In this chapter, our focus will be on how to improve the skills that would eventually improve your ability to generate humor. Humor in any form requires your command over vocabulary because the number of ideas in your head is relative to the size of your word bank. The second step is to boost your intelligence, which will ensure that you have a keen sense of observation. Learning how to use pun is the next step, followed by mastering the art of conversation, which is a must to deliver humor in the best manner possible.

Building Vocabulary

The beginning of a new school year always meant that it was the time to get new books. One thing I have always observed was that, the new books had numerous new words, which were more difficult than those in the previous ones. This simply means that, with each increasing school year I was being taught of words I never knew before and this meant more hectic word drills and eventually, a bigger word bank.

The emphasis on vocabulary building is an important aspect of our education system. The testing systems all around the world rely on gauging a student's vocabulary to judge his or her potential. This whole preamble about the importance of vocabulary leads to one question, "Why is building vocabulary so important?" The answer to this question lies in understanding the basic concept that words express ideas and the more words you know, the more capable you are in conveying your ideas exactly the way you thought them to be.

This concept is completely valid for those who are seeking to gain command over humor. Humor is basically a presentation of ideas that would seem funny to the audience. These ideas need to be presented in a manner wherein they would not lose their funny aspect. This means that the choice of words is more important in the case of humor. It is not about just conveying a certain message; it is more about preserving the essence of humor through the use of precise words. As it is settled that building vocabulary is essential for gaining command over humor, the next step is to learn how to build a vast and diverse vocabulary suited to our needs.

For many of us, school is over and there will be nobody giving us word drills. With that option exhausted, we need to focus on our reading habits. Words are all around us, they are present in every form of printed material, books, magazines, newspapers, online blogs, websites, and articles. The only source of getting across new words is to read more and more. Identify each new word, look up the meaning, and absorb the word in its context.

Successfully building vocabulary through this process requires a lot of discipline and patience. A person needs to realize that there is no quick way to building a vast vocabulary; it can only be done in small steps. A few words each day and every day will ensure a bigger word bank each month, a vast one by the end of the year, and after a few years you will be mastering the language in a manner that you yourself will be astonished by the progress you made.

The most important thing for anyone who is seeking to build vocabulary is to possess and keep in handy a good dictionary. It is the most valuable asset in your arsenal. The purpose of keeping a dictionary is for consultation whenever you come across a new word. Developing a habit to immediately find meanings for unknown words will enable you to learn the meaning of the word in the context it is being used.

Other than using the dictionary for finding the meaning of new words, reading the dictionary also helps a lot in building vocabulary. All the entries, which are unfamiliar, will pique the interest of the reader and the dictionary along with providing meanings of words also gives insight on the origins and usage of these words.

The next best tool is the thesaurus. A thesaurus not only helps you in finding alternate words, but it also assists you in finding the most suitable word that you need to use. Using a thesaurus on a regular basis will broaden your horizons about the language under study, making you understand the difference in the usage of certain words. There can be numerous words to describe one thing, but each context requires that a different yet most suitable word is to be used.

Building vocabulary involves an extraordinary work ethic. It begins with setting achievable goals. One cannot memorize and learn twenty new words every day. Setting up such a goal will not only diminish your interest in building your vocabulary, but it will also be counterproductive.

Find the number of words you can easily remember and then stick to it until you reach the point when you are capable of learning more words in a given period. Practical application of your learning is a-must to retain words in your vocabulary. To do that, you should regularly write and ensure the usage of new words, which you have learned. Taking aid from memorization techniques such as the flash cards and post-it notes is a very good idea. These techniques are developed solely for the purpose of memorization and will assist you in a manner where you will be amazed at the results you were able to achieve.

Last, but not the least, learning a little Latin would do wonders for your vocabulary building. Most of the English words have their origins from the Latin language. Learning about the roots of these words in Latin can help you find the meanings of words that you haven't memorized yet, but have Latin origins.

Boost Your Intelligence

Good humor is a product of a brilliant mind because it involves astute observation, out of the box thinking, and a clever connection between various ideas. This means that boosting your intelligence is a major component when learning to be humorous. Intelligence is usually measured in terms of Intelligence Quotient (IQ) derived from the results of tests that involve problem solving, spatial imagery, memory, general knowledge, and other components. There are studies that indicate an improvement in the intelligence level makes it possible for you to boost up your mind, thereby bringing it to a level that will enable you to become more humorous.

The most effective way to achieve something is to make the process more enjoyable. Finding fun in improving your brain power will give you results beyond imagination. For this purpose, one should try playing games such as Scrabble and Sudoku for brain exercise. Nevertheless, do not be limited to these since these are not the only games that can hone your mental capacity. So, expand your horizons. Once you have achieved mastery in any of the skills you are honing such as word-building in Scrabble, you can then start honing other skills such as numbering skill by playing Sudoku.

Research has revealed that during the initial stages of skill development the brain consumes more glucose than in the later stages where one has mastered the skill. This indicates that the brain needs to put in more effort when it is learning something new. But, when it has been learned and you have adapted to the level of difficulty, things get easier for the brain. This might mean that there is no more room for growth. In order to boost our intelligence, we should find new ways to challenge our brain.

Stimulating the brain is extremely important for boosting intelligence. Video games are great stimulation sources. However, one should always try to play games that are out of the range of usual choices. This will enable you to work on the weaker areas of the brain as well as practice skills that you have not mastered yet. This will also force you to find solutions to problems, which have been left unanswered. Constantly challenging your brain is extremely important. As the saying, "No pain, no gain" is true for bodybuilders, it is also equally true in terms of building up your brain power.

One can never separate their physical existence from their mental state. A fit and healthy body can only support a healthy mind. It is scientifically proven that to enhance your brain power, you have to keep your body fit. Exercising the body is the best way to ensure both physical and mental health. What would happen if I say you are forced to sit in an office chair for long hours? The most logical answer is that you will start gaining weight, lose the strength of your muscles that are not being used, and might end up having back problems from sitting in the same posture.

This happens to our brain, too! Applying our mental abilities in working out limited kinds of issues and problems makes us lose strength in the unused areas of our brain. To avoid such a situation, one must diversify their tastes. For instance, learn to paint well, or study art and architecture. The more diverse things you learn, the more your intelligence will grow.

Interacting with society also enables the growth of intelligence. This might sound illogical, but the mechanism behind this is that, the exposure to the community can in turn expose your mind to new ideas, beliefs, and notions. This new information will be at times in contradiction to your existing ideas, beliefs, and notions.

There can be two reactions to this new information - rejection or adaptation. Your mind may strengthen the existing beliefs, thereby rejecting the information or it may grow and adopt the new information it has discovered. Observation plays a very important role in boosting intelligence. Looking at things with a different perspective and being aware of the happenings at a higher level is essential for being smart. This can be learned through practice and expansive observation.

Use of Pun

Merriam-Webster defines pun as "the usually humorous use of a word in such a way as to suggest two or more of its meanings or the meaning of another word similar in sound." This definition of pun suggests that it has something to do with creative wordplay, which pushes the boundaries of context as well as includes the wanted humor in whatever you are trying to say.

Understanding the anatomy of a pun is very important because puns possess an indirect correlation to a certain context. This correlation is the basis of the humor that puns intend to achieve. Puns usually involve words that may sound alike and they may or may not rhyme. Precise use of pun comes after an extensive understanding and study of the language.

Noticing words, which are read and heard daily as well as making creative connections between the hidden relationships they have with certain subjects and contexts is the main core of puns. The point is to discover these hidden relationships despite the fact that they are completely separate on the surface.

Understanding a pun is just the first part of a two-piece puzzle. The second and most important part is the impeccable delivery, which involves perfect timing of pun in the conversation. To learn how to do this one, you first need to become a keen listener. Only by listening with intent can a listener identify the opportunity when it is presented. Pun can be admitted in to any conversation after extensive practice and gaining the required expertise.

Chapter 5: Mastering the Art of Conversation

This book has been written with an aim to help people use humor as a tool for social acceptability. This means that the audience of this book is looking forward to introducing humor in their conversations so that others may find them funny, likeable, and friendly. Mastering the art of conversation is a key foundation to delivering humor that would make people roll with laughter.

Before we divulge into how to be an expert conversationalist, we should identify what makes a conversation successful. When we are talking to a person we are close with, for example a friend, we measure the success of the conversation by how enthralled we were by what the other person said. However, this changes completely when we are talking to a stranger. In conversations with strangers, the topic of the conversation is usually trivial and we rate the success of conversation through our own performance.

I have no authority to tell people how to talk to friends for they would know you better and you are not intending to impress them with your conversational skills. It is when we are with unfamiliar people that we need to utilize the tools we are about to learn right now. The first step to a conversation is to make sure that you keep in mind these five basic principles.

First, put others at ease. Make them feel comfortable in the conversation so that they will actually listen to what you have to say. Second, put yourself at ease. Make yourself calm so that you can fully indulge in the experience. Third, involve all the parties. If there are people who are not part of this conversation, they will lose interest and will start up their own conversation, which is not at all good. Fourth, identify shared interests. The more quickly you identify shared interest, the more quickly you will be able to steer the conversation, which attracts attention from everyone around. Last, actively pursue your own conversation.

Every conversation begins with an introduction. Keeping it small is the only rule of introduction. An introduction must address two things: "Who we are?" and "Why are we relevant?" Any other information will be extraneous. After introduction, you need to make the conversation progress.

The conversation must be incremental and these steps are laid out courtesies followed by trade information then trade opinion and then trade feeling. To make sure you are a good conversationalist, follow this basic rule, "Good conversationalists listen more than they talk." This would allow you to hear what people are really saying than what they are telling. Both these things are quite different as directness is a privilege of intimacy and people you have met just now will not say things to you directly. In order to get what people mean, you need to derive it from what they are telling you. Nothing ruins a conversation more than a bad ending. To close a conversation amicably you must ease in by starting your sentence with "Lastly..." or "Finally..." indicating that this is the last thing you need to say. Farewell can also be implied by telling them you don't want to keep them from doing important tasks or by saying that it was a pleasant conversation.

Conclusion

Thank you again for downloading this book!

I hope this book was able to help you learn the art of humor by understanding the basic elements of humor, by differentiating between its various forms, and by explaining to you the various skills that must be developed.

The next step is to implement all that you have learned in this book in your day-to-day lives and then reap the benefits humor has to offer.

Finally, if you enjoyed this book, please take the time to share your thoughts and post a review on Amazon. It'd be greatly appreciated!

Thank you and good luck!

Made in the USA
Middletown, DE
08 May 2015